Baby Learns to Lean

by Matthew Grizzle

I'm not a psychologist. I am a dad trying to help his family and others thrive in the midst of big life changes and I hope what we are learning could help you as well.

Baby Learns to Lean
Copyright © 2026 by Matthew Grizzle

The views and opinions expressed in this book are those of the author and do not necessarily reflect the official policy or position of Illumify Media Global.
Published by
Illumify Media Global
www.IllumifyMedia.com
"Let's bring your book to life!"
Paperback ISBN: 978-1-970582-00-0

Cover design by Debbie Lewis

Printed in the United States of America

To the many counselors, teachers, mentors, and friends who have helped my wife and I understand the need for emotional connection, the value of giving that to our son, and above all, helping us learn how to lean on one another

In the beginning baby is born and mommy gets a superpower she didn't have before: to comfort and soothe, to hold and to feed until the day baby can learn how to lean.

4

To welcome this life is a gift without lack.
It's the yummy, and warm, daily booya snack.
But when baby grows, mommy's milk goes,
Till one day it doesn't come back.

Then one day mommy will look at baby and say "Booboos are closed starting today."

Baby starts to cry, How can I sleep? What did I do? What does it mean?"

I know you are sad and how hard this will be, but now we get the gift of learning how to lean.

"Lean? What is that? Baby asks.

What do I do? How do I learn to lean into you?"

Change the world

Leaning is a gift that God gives to you,
              One that we keep and forever we use.
First you look deep in my eyes,
              Take my hands and see me smile.

I pick you up, and nuzzle your nose.
We hold each other and look real close.
We sing our songs,
say our prayers,
Take deep breaths,
and don't forget
the
stares...

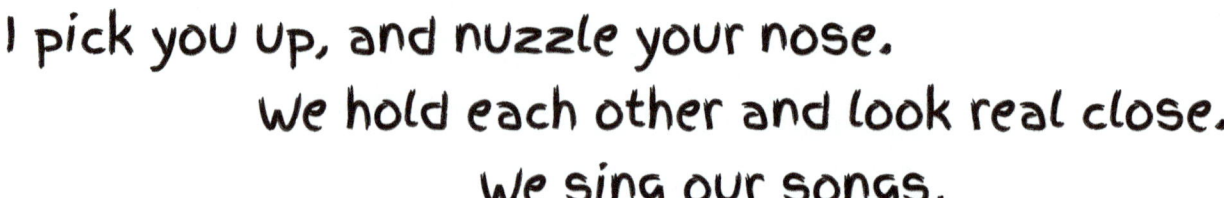

Baby Le
to L

Not the kind you climb up and down,
but eyes that are tied, not looking around.
One final kiss cradled on my knees,
Then off to bed with

one... last...

twenty-second squeeze.

Good night, baby.
Sweet dreams, my sweet.
Close your eyes.
It's time for sleep.

Leaning Chart

Let your child add a mark or sticker to each day as you lean on each other.

21 Days ✓ **Naptime Leaning**

| 1 | 2 | 3 | 4 | 5 | 6 | 7 |

| 8 | 9 | 10 | 11 | 12 | 13 | 14 |

| 15 | 16 | 17 | 18 | 19 | 20 | 21 |

21 Days ✓ **Bedtime Leaning**

| 1 | 2 | 3 | 4 | 5 | 6 | 7 |

| 8 | 9 | 10 | 11 | 12 | 13 | 14 |

| 15 | 16 | 17 | 18 | 19 | 20 | 21 |

Note from the Author

You have labored for this day and now it has arrived. I imagine it is a blend of emotions, just as it was for us. We encourage you to have a special celebration to commemorate the transition. We called it Leaning Day, and we had a special breakfast with a candle and even a gift prepared for our son. A celebration is a wonderful way to help the whole family end this journey together and it felt like a coming-of-age ceremony. Included is a special page to journal about what you did and how you made it special. I hope it becomes a memory you look back on and treasure for many years to come. And don't forget to take a picture for such a huge milestone. Well done! Please read to the end for what were some helpful tips for our family along the way, as well as a personal note from my wife—mom to mom.

Leaning Day Memories

_____

_____

_____

_____

_____

_____

_____

_____

Preparation

Research supports that this is key in helping them mentally and emotionally prepare for transition, and there are creative ways to do it.

Tip: Reading the book together and talking about it are great ways you can start introducing your child to the idea. Do this even for a few weeks beforehand to give them time to process the transition coming.

Tip: Schedule a few opportunities to practice where mommy is gone for nap time or bedtime and baby must lean on daddy. We did this maybe three or four times before cutting out naptime feedings. We didn't cut nighttime feedings until three weeks later.

Routine

Having a routine is incredibly important in a child's development. Consider how best to fit in this new concept to your already existing bedtime routine. If you do not have one, consider researching some simple routines to make bedtime more enjoyable for everyone.

Tip: As with any transition, it can be challenging at first but trusting the process and being consistent will help your child know what to expect which in turn will gradually help them adapt. Give time to establish a routine and don't make too many changes at once.

Tip: Taking a parenting course was a huge help to us!

Stares

Looking into each other's eyes and smiling is a fantastic way to build connection and intimacy. The brain releases several endorphins that help one to feel connected. You stare for a few seconds, then close your eyes or look away. Stare at each other again when you're ready and repeat as many times as you want.

Tip: Your child likely will not want to sit still for prolonged periods of time for this so discovering a playful way of approaching this activity can be immensely helpful. One way is letting them direct when to open and close their eyes, and another way is using a comfort blanket to play a version of peek-a-boo. This not only lets your child enjoy the process of connecting with you, but you too will feel more connection with them.

Tip: You don't have to smile the whole time! When you look away or close your eyes, take a breath and relax until you look into your child's eyes again. Research suggests that smiling after making eye contact versus smiling before eye contact impacts the brain differently, with the former being more beneficial.

Tip: It is very important for your child to experience you delighting in them in a focused manner consistently. As you smile while you look at them, It will be small glimpses of what you used to feel before they were weaned. And be encouraged that though the connection is different, it is good for both of you.

Deep breaths

Whether while holding their hands, snuggled up close, or during a hug, deep abdominal breathing is important for settling as it relaxes the body.

Tip: The best thing is if you are holding your child closely, they will subconsciously mirror you as you regulate your own breathing. Plus, it keeps you calm if they are a little rowdier. But do whatever works for you two.

Tip: Don't worry if they are moving around or can't sit still. Your calm presence does more than you think. Consider setting a snuggle timer (with a gentle alarm) to let them know when it will be over.

Tip: Don't stress about the order of these things! It's not an algorithm as much as giving you tools to protect and build healthy emotional attachment. For example, we start with stares, then snuggle as we do more of our bedtime routine.

The Twenty-Second Squeeze

A hug lasting at least twenty seconds has an immensely beneficial impact on your body's ability to relax due to the production of oxytocin and serotonin.

Tip: Turn it into a countdown timer where you count together. It makes a great final step before putting them in the crib or bed.

Tip: Can be done standing, or sitting, so if your child has a preference, do that.

Tip: Do it as a family group hug if you can. I know that isn't always possible but it can be a great reassurance to your child and it might become a special moment for all of you. But if your child is like mine and resists, you don't have to force it. It sure is special though, when we are all a part of it.

Other Tips

Tip: Children like to test boundaries. Decide ahead of time what you will do and stick to it. Know that if they make a "small" suggestion, it may seem small in the moment but recognize they may be attempting to build on the routine to keep it fresh. Think about It before saying yes because it is easier to say no when they first suggest it than to do it a few times then start saying no because you changed your mind.

Tip: Consider a small reward like a sticker for completing leaning each time. It can also be a helpful reminder to them if they are delaying things or not really following your lead through the process.

Tip: Our two-year old son loved sleeping with "stuffies," so we had to limit him through making them rewards for the bedtime routine and leaning.

Tip: We have used things like sticker charts or letting him mark a checklist since the beginning and found that to be helpful with our son. After a certain number of stickers, we give him a little prize and they don't have to be monetary to be helpful. If it is something your child enjoys, then it will motivate them. But if stickers don't work for you try something else.

Tip: It can be an emotional roller coaster as your hormones are changing on top of the emotional transition that is taking place. This is totally normal, but it may also be helpful to look into counseling or therapy as you process the change yourself.

Tip: Lean on your spouse. Practice these things as a couple, and when you feel distressed, lean on each other. Whether it is specifically related to the weaning transition or not, it can be a bonding experience for you too.

Mom to mom

There's no "right" way to feel about weaning. Some moms look forward to it, others dread it, and many of us feel a little bit of everything. I'll be honest—when my son turned two, just thinking about weaning brought me to tears. It's such a tender transition, and it's okay if your heart feels pulled in different directions.

If you're not ready, or your little one isn't ready, don't let anyone rush you. You truly can nurse as long as it feels right for you both. When you are ready, it can help to choose a date for your final nursing session—but even then, don't be surprised if you second-guess yourself when that day arrives. I certainly did.

After our "leaning day," my son still asked to nurse for a while, and each time tugged at my heart. But a gentle reminder was all he needed, and within a month he stopped asking. What surprised me most was how different closeness felt afterward. Nursing had always held his full attention, but learning to lean, snuggle, or simply be still together was a new skill for both of us.

If this season stirs up grief or mixed emotions, you're not alone. Talk to your spouse, a friend, or someone you trust. Lean on your people while you teach your little one how to lean on you in new ways. You're doing beautifully, Mama—truly.

www.ingramcontent.com/pod-product-compliance
Lightning Source LLC
Chambersburg PA
CBHW051629140626
46547CB00033B/2978